My Endless Journey

A memoir about mourning and music

By Kathryn R Bennett

First published by Kathryn R Bennett in 2023
eighteenallornothing@gmail.com
ISBN 978-0-6488876-2-1 (Paperback)
Cover design by Judith M Bennett
Internal design & typesetting by Rack and Rune Publishing.
Immortalising Joy reprinted with kind permission from
Justine Nguyen and Musica Viva.

This book is dedicated to
Jennifer Claire Bates,
in whose honour Endless *was*
composed and performed.

Part 1

A Commission

I finger my earrings distractedly as I sit in the light-filled Lutheran Church on Melbourne's South Bank. A concert is about to begin. In the pew beside me is my sister Judith. A few dozen other guests occupy the timber benches, but it is by no means a large gathering. In fact, it is a "house concert", a gift from the Flinders Quartet to a subscriber of Radio 3MBS to play for a private audience at a venue of the host's choosing. It was Maryanne's name that was drawn from the proverbial hat as the lucky winner, and this church was Maryanne's selection of venue. As the commissioner of *Endless*, a piece that will receive its first performance today, Maryanne sent me a special invitation via Musica Viva.

As I trace the metal edges of my earrings I am transported to Bhutan. With my daughter Jennifer I am in a gift shop in Thimphu with its myriad items of Buddhist symbolism - from etched brass singing bowls that summon spiritual contemplation, to carved wooden erect penises that invoke fertility. The symbol that most resonated with Jen and me was the eternal or endless knot, not dissimilar to some Celtic knots that Jen used to draw as a child when connecting with her part-Irish ancestry. As one of the six Buddhist symbols it is widely depicted in temples and as an architectural decoration on domestic and public buildings. We were both drawn to the endless knot for its representation of interconnectedness across all dimensions – time, space, life. I was not to know then that 26 months later it would include that tragic dimension of death; Jennifer's death.

My trip to Bhutan was special on many levels. Jen and her husband Jordi had already been there for half of their twelve-month assignment as volunteer development ambassadors for the Australian Government. Jordi was the official volunteer, working on water infrastructure projects. Jen, a registered architect and project manager, independently volunteered her skills across a range of projects, including a Centre for Gross National Happiness, a women's refuge and the inaugural Thimphu Cultural Festival. Their apartment in Thimphu could accommodate a mattress on the living room floor for the duration of my visit, enabling me to avoid the strict and expensive Bhutanese visa system that requires tourists to pay not only for accommodation but for the personal services of both a guide and a driver. In this way Bhutan limits the number of tourists and addresses the sustainability of their tourist industry without it draining their food supply or infrastructure capacities. Mine was a special visa, one of only two allocated to Jen and Jordi for the duration of their stay, and only available after they had been there for six months. At the first opportunity I flew into Paro airport, the most challenging landing strip of any commercial airline, with only eight pilots qualified to make this "tricky landing" as described at the time by Jen. It felt like we almost clipped the mountain sides on the approach through the steep valley, with a right-angle turn just before landing. For the next three weeks Jen would be my personal guide, the best I could ever wish for.

Since 2001 Jen and I have taken special holidays together, on average every two to three years. We started in 2001 with a camping tour of Australia's red centre, then an Intrepid tour of Vietnam, Cambodia and Thailand, and another time we relaxed together in Vanuatu. When she made her first trip as an Australian Government volunteer to the Philippines in 2006, I was invited to join her for Christmas. When Jen's contract ended, Jordi still had three months to the completion of his assignment in Vietnam, and Jen was able to extend her leave from work to join him there. Again I was invited, this time to share a trekking trip with her in the Sapa region. So the Bhutan visit was the latest in a long line of special times we shared overseas. We took in cultural festivals, mountain treks, and shared hot stone baths full of mountain herbs. Neither of us then knew that this would be our last adventure together.

As part of her immersion in Bhutanese culture Jen explored Buddhism, its philosophy and symbolism. She wrote about it in the online blog she published throughout her stay. On her return home she held on to some of those aspects, like her morning yoga practice and meditation to reduce stress. She also retained her connection with the endless knot using its design to create ceramic tiles that she crafted in her evening pottery class.

All this was my rush of reflection that filled the few seconds before the musicians walked onto the Lutheran Church stage. My fingertips caressed each silver square to reinforce my sense of connection with Jen. Back in the Thimphu gift shop, choosing the silver earrings, while trying not to look at the erect timber penises, I could not have known just how significant a symbol this would become.

Ever since it happened, on the morning of 14 December 2016, I have tried hard not to focus on the circumstances of Jennifer's death, but rather on the life she lived. It continues to surprise me that rather than anger towards the young man who took my daughter's life by his reckless driving, I hold out hope that he can turn his life into something meaningful both for him and others. He has now served his time in jail, a short four years, the remaining three of his sentence to be served on parole. I choose not to contemplate the concepts of justice, fairness or due retribution. Jennifer's life will never be restored, no matter how this fellow is punished, yet his future actions have the capacity to help the world rather than damage it, should he choose to take that path. That is my wish.

Because of his actions my world changed for ever. Jen and I were each other's best friends, our texting term of endearment being MFF (My Favourite Female). In the most practical of terms, losing my only child meant that I needed to change my Will (and my Enduring Guardian, but that's another matter entirely). By the time I could contemplate such matters the world was in Covid lockdown. Among other things my attendance at concerts came to a halt. In particular, I was missing the Musica Viva concerts that brought musicians of the world to my back door in Newcastle. As a long-time subscriber I highly value the opportunity to hear live chamber music in a hall that suits it so well, the Newcastle Conservatorium. My heart went out to musicians whose livelihoods were severely impacted by cancellation of performances and, like many, I forfeited my subscription fees to help them in the small way I could.

With these thoughts in mind I considered the alternative recipients of what might be left of my estate upon my death. Naturally Musica Viva was high on the list. But it was inspiration generated by Jennifer's loss that sent me in a different direction. Rather than wait until I die, why not do something now? And instead of it being about me, why not let this be one of my ways to honour Jen? And so I set out on what I now describe as my *Endless* journey.

Though I attend concerts and listen to classical music a lot, I am by no means musically educated - other than scraping a bow across violin strings at school and trying to pass my Grade 3 piano exam. The fact that I never mastered the art of reading music meant that I never progressed. So it was from a position of complete ignorance that I developed the idea of commissioning a piece of music. In an action that I still find hard to recognise as mine, I made a stab-in-the-dark approach to an Australian composer with whom I share the tragic loss of a child. Grief has a knack of adding significance to certain pieces of music. One such for me is *Compassion* by Nigel Westlake, its musical representation of compassion as depicted in different religions resonating with how Jen and I embraced some of the Buddhist teachings. As I understand it, *Compassion* was a work undertaken by Mr Westlake by way of coming to terms with his son Eli's death. I felt that perhaps he may be the person I could approach for my commission.

I was humbled to receive a personal email response from Mr Westlake rather than his publicist. He not only provided me with helpful advice but also expressed his deep understanding of my loss. Unable to take on the commission himself he gave me what would turn out to be the best suggestion. He recommended that I approach Musica Viva. My understanding of Musica Viva at that stage did not include involvement in commissioning new music, a further example of the naivety of my starting point.

In early 2021 Musica Viva concerts were able to go ahead, showcasing Australian musicians rather than attracting overseas artistes. By that time the Newcastle Conservatorium was closed for renovations. Like many organisations, the University of Newcastle used Covid lockdowns as an opportunity for capital works. As a result, Musica Viva concerts relocated to Newcastle City Hall, and in March I was delighted to be among a small, masked and socially distanced audience to hear oboist Diana Doherty perform with the Streeton Trio.

It was at a meeting over lunch the day after that concert when I met Katherine, Zoe and Caroline, representatives of Musica Viva, for my first ever conversation about how a commission might work. In the months that followed, the stars aligned in many ways, the significance of which I couldn't fully understand until the concert performances were under way. The Flinders Quartet and Karin Schaupp had already been contracted by Musica Viva for a concert tour in February/March 2022. I learned that "for over 20 years" the internationally acclaimed guitarist, Karin Schaupp had wanted Carl Vine to write something for her to perform. Following Carl's departure as Artistic Director of Musica Viva his successor, Paul Kildea, wanted the organisation to honour him by commissioning a work. My approach to Musica Viva, to commission 'something', occurred right at this point. That everything else had already been established could not have worked more to my advantage. It almost felt as if my request slotted in as the keystone, locking everything else in place.

By June 2021 we were back in Covid lockdowns, so I first spoke with Carl Vine and Paul Kildea through my laptop in a Zoom meeting. Everyone was on board for a piece to be written for Karin Schaupp and the Flinders Quartet to be premiered in the first program of 2022. I exchanged contact details with Carl, and sent him some background information about Jen. In fact he had already done some research and discovered her Bhutan blog. He was also aware of how her life had ended. One of my criteria for the piece was that it would be uplifting, not morbid. Not knowing quite how far I could be prescriptive, I also asked if some salsa rhythms could be included, explaining how Jen and Jordi had met at salsa classes, and danced an amazing wedding salsa at their reception in 2011. Carl and I developed an email connection that was unexpected on my part, and, as I came to understand, also appreciated by Carl. I sent him links, photos and videos, and even shared with him Jennifer's book *Eighteen* that I was at that point still editing. It was a pleasant surprise that the composer was willing to receive this information. Little did I realise just how strong an advocate Carl would become for Jen, nor how beautifully he would capture her essence in his music.

In late October 2021 Musica Viva published their program for 2022. They were hopeful to "bring audiences back to concert halls in Australia" [Musica Viva Australia, 26 October 2021]. It was my first opportunity to see the reality of my adventure, to see in print the reference to my commission. The Musica Viva program referred to the yet-to-be-named piece as:

> *"a brand new Australian work commissioned by Paul Kildea from his predecessor Carl Vine AO. This new commission immortalises the joyous memory of a Musica Viva subscriber's late daughter".*

Now it felt real. Now there were butterflies in my stomach. I had a date to pin the world premiere performance to

– Thursday 24 February at Llewellyn Hall in Canberra. I would be there with bells on!

Between the Zoom meeting in June and 29 November when Carl completed the score, our email communication extended my learning curve dramatically. It was initially surprising, yet deeply gratifying, that Carl was including me in a swathe of issues connected to his creative processes. He shared with me his plans to collaborate with Karin Schaupp since, not having written for guitar before, he needed to discuss 'technical aspects' with her. He introduced me to the publishing process and its practice to include a Program Note. Not only did Carl share that draft with me, but also invited my comments, making adaptations accordingly. He also included me in the selection of a title for the piece. Having put forward a few alternatives we both agreed that "Endless", Carl's suggestion, would be most appropriate.

And then in December 2021 I received a postal delivery of the score! There, on the front page was a huge image of an endless knot, above which were Carl's name and the simple title: ENDLESS. On the inside page was another endless knot below the text box containing the Program Note:

> *This work celebrates the life of Jennifer Bates, a*
> *professional architect, project manager and dedicated*

It fills me with awe today as I re-read it, just as it did when I saw it in print for the first time. The depth of the dedication to Jen is beyond my dreams. That these aspects of her life will be eternally connected with this piece of music is a legacy greater than my commission. It is indeed a "living legacy for a precious life that ended too soon."

From one surprise to another, the online program for Musica Viva 2022 contained more cause for my heart to race. Each concert throughout the year receives its own description with details of the music to be performed. The entry for Karin Schaupp & Flinders Quartet was as follows:

> *Once in a while a collaboration reaches the heart of why we make music. This concert honours such a collaboration, built on friendship and love.*
>
> *Composer Carl Vine was for two decades Musica Viva Australia's artistic director. In 2019 Paul Kildea assumed the mantle, and for this concert asked his predecessor to create a new work for a much-admired soloist and string quartet, commissioned by a longstanding subscriber wishing to immortalise the joyous memory of her late daughter.*

The tour dates were advertised as 20 February to 12 March 2022. However, the pandemic had another agenda. Just two weeks before the anticipated world premiere performance of *Endless* the concert tour was postponed. Covid numbers were in resurgence and protection of the musicians was paramount. This became even more significant when I learned that one of the performers has a health compromise.

I don't remember being devastated by this decision. I think our experiences through lockdowns, and the overwhelming statistics of deaths related to Covid, brought with them a capacity to adapt and accept the almost daily changes to how we conducted our lives. I took solace in the decision by Musica Viva not to cancel, but to postpone, and held on to the hope that a year later would bring different circumstances and enable the concert to open their 2023 series instead. I was also relieved that the immune-compromised musician was not unduly put at risk.

Was it a long twelve months of waiting? Did it dampen my enthusiasm for *Endless?* Did it feel like another loss? Actually, no. By chance I was heavily absorbed by another project in honour of Jennifer – the editing and publishing of her book *Eighteen.*

The year Jennifer turned eighteen she was living in Poland as a Rotary Youth Exchange student. For twelve months she kept a diary of her experiences. It was always her intention to publish it on her return to Australia, but then her architecture studies, work, living life and meeting Jordi all took her away from the task. It is another of my blessings to have been able to achieve publication on Jen's behalf. I titled Jen's book *Eighteen,* its subtitle *All or Nothing* a reference to one of the mottos she held for the year of her exchange. Eighteen years later that vibrant life, full of learning and living, was extinguished. In June, on what would have been Jen's 42nd birthday, I took the first printed copies of *Eighteen, All or Nothing* to a small family gathering at her graveside. We toasted Jen and the successful publication of her memoir. By October I was focussed on launching the book.

The concert in Melbourne's Lutheran Church is about to begin. The program comprises most of the works that will be played on the Musica Viva tour, this concert being a sort of rehearsal. The piece I am most looking forward to hearing, *Endless*, is second on the list. I allow the Carulli guitar concerto to wash over me as my mind races, filled with everything that has led to this moment. It will be the first time anyone has heard this particular combination of notes, other than the musicians who are about to play it. Not even the composer, Carl Vine, has heard it played on the instruments for which he has composed it. Although I've received the *Endless* manuscript my incapacity to read the music (which incidentally includes notation marks that are quite unfamiliar to me) means that its mystery has remained intact, - until now.

It is hard to describe my initial reaction. Without Carl's subsequent explanation I was left to make my own interpretation of the unfamiliar sounds. My head and my heart competed with each other to find meaning.

Afterwards I was unable to remember much of what I had heard. Instead the earworm I took home that afternoon was the familiar Boccherini *Fandango* with which the concert ended. What I do recall is a beam of light that pierced a high stained-glass window in the church just as the salsa rhythm emerged from Carl's composition. My eyes filled with tears as I imagined Jen's dainty ankles and her dancing feet.

I had practiced remembering the names of the musicians; Thibaud (first violin), Wilma (second violin), Helen (viola), Zoe (cello), and of course Karin on guitar. I had prepared a card and endless knot gift for each of them as a token of my appreciation - a stainless-steel pin for Thibaud, and silver necklaces for the women. Zoe immediately wore hers, and I have not seen her without it ever since.

As she emerged from backstage, Karin Schaupp made a beeline for me. Her first words "Can I give you a hug?" were a surprise and a delight. Not only was social distancing not required, but the social divide between world-renowned guitarist and anonymous me was swept away. As one who enjoys giving and receiving hugs, my immediate thought was "Oh, she's on my wavelength!" Later Karin would share with me that she felt an instant connection with me, a privilege I will treasure for ever.

Meeting Thibaud, Wilma, Helen and Zoe, the

members of the Flinders Quartet together with Karin, and seeing how comfortably they interacted with each other, and now with me, relieved me of my insecurities and that ingrained British notion of class division. Here were five people who had made Jennifer's acquaintance through music and were talking about her in the present tense. There could be no more meaningful gift to a bereft mother.

Though the world was gradually opening up after the pandemic lockdowns, Covid still had a sting in the tail. At Christmas my sister Judith endured a bad dose of it, among another upsurge of numbers. So in January 2023 I was again very nervous about the viability of the tour. My concerns once more focussed on the health of the musicians and the impact on audience numbers. At the same time I wanted to hear *Endless* as many times as possible, and planned to attend the whole of the concert tour. With some hesitation I started booking flights and accommodation for each of the concert venues, four State capital cities as well as Canberra. Part of my intrigue was to learn about how musicians approach the arduous nature of a three-week performance tour, and wondered if I might glimpse an insight into this from the sidelines. In fact what I experienced was the sweeping away of sidelines and a total sense of inclusivity.

One of my aims in commissioning the music was to

create an opportunity to introduce Jennifer to others. Never could I have imagined how deep this introduction could become, nor from so many diverse directions. My own limited concept was to provide the gift of a bookmark to each concert patron. I arranged with Musica Viva that their personnel and/or the venue staff would assist with the distribution process, and I delivered bundles to each venue just before the concert. For its design I chose the beautiful photo that I took of Jen in Bhutan, wearing her new kira and sash when we were on our way to a temple festival. On the back of the bookmark I added references to her published works - the blogs she wrote when in Bhutan and the Philippines, as well as her book *Eighteen, All or Nothing*.

Carl's advocacy for Jen was quite unanticipated. Though he derived much information about her from her Bhutan blog, I did not expect that he would invite others to read it. He referred to it each time he made his stage presentation prior to the performance of *Endless*. On his personal website he has created a hotlink to it, and through the publishers of his manuscript, Faber, another link appears in their magazine *Faber Music Performance News* in an article announcing the publication of *Endless*.

Another champion of Jen, with his support of *Eighteen* as well as *Endless,* is Scott Bevan. Scott, a Newcastle based journalist and radio presenter, interviewed me as well as Carl prior to the Newcastle concert. He spoke with Carl by phone, but he met me in Civic Park, directly opposite City Hall. As I turned toward the fountain I had a flashback to 1984 when my three-year-old daughter, newly arrived in Australia, was captured in a photo sitting beside the dancing water. That same fountain now provided the background to my interview with Scott, as did the raucous galahs. Looking across at the City Hall I imagined my 36-year-old daughter who had filled its hall just months before her death. As a leader of an environment group she orchestrated a forum for renewable energy there which was so popular that a second event had to be scheduled. I wondered if she might fill the hall again for the *Endless* concert.

As an ABC journalist Scott Bevan put together our interviews for broadcast on ABC Newcastle, and it went to air on the Friday before the concert. It had been my privilege to connect with Scott when I was preparing *Eighteen* for publication. Indeed the book bears his endorsement on the back cover. Scott had also graciously accepted my invitation to chair the October book launch at Hunter Sports High School. I selected the venue as being most appropriate for the book launch as Jen was project manager for the redevelopment of the school. She had met with then Deputy Principal (now Principal) Rachel Byrne, several times a week in the previous couple of years. They enjoyed a fruitful and respectful working relationship, despite the many challenges of such a large project. The day the building works were due to begin was the day Jen's life was taken, giving her boss Drew Varnum the unimaginable task of finding a substitute project manager while handling his own intense grief. He and Jen had a wonderful working relationship and Jen often told me of Drew's sage advice, listening ear and encouragement of her professional development. His eulogy at Jen's funeral was a testament to his deep respect for her. He was instrumental in creating an annual award in Jennifer's name for the Department of Regional New South Wales, the government department under which Public Works now sits. Each year I am invited to present the award to a young female who shows potential for leadership, just like Jen did. Each year at the presentation, Drew's voice breaks when he introduces the reason behind the award. At the 2022 Award presentation I discovered that, as young boys, Drew and Scott played cricket together. Those endless interconnections!

Other media outlets also covered the *Endless* story. Articles in *Limelight* and *Sydney Arts magazine* about the music included generous references to Jen. In addition to Scott's interview for ABC Newcastle, Radio 3MBS interviewed the Flinders Quartet cellist, Zoe Knighton and included a reference to Jen. What was most surprising, however, was the two-page spread at the back of every Musica Viva program for the concert tour, both the printed versions distributed at each venue as well as the online version emailed to subscribers. In a section titled *Stories to Inspire* Justine Nguyen wrote a piece about *Endless* that she called *Immortalising Joy*. I couldn't have chosen a more fitting title to represent my intentions for this commission, and I thank Justine for her inspiration. She also used the same smiling image of Jennifer in her Bhutanese kira that seems to leap off the page and describe joy itself.

The endless knot has become our symbol for Jennifer. It is inlaid in brass at the kerbside where her life was taken, and carved into her memorial stone close to where her body lies in a natural burial site at Ryhope. One of her red-glazed ceramic tiles adorns the wall in my study, and I made a cushion bearing its design to occupy the seat between my sister Judith and me for the Newcastle concert. I wanted Jen to have her own space for that special occasion.

Both in our 70's Judith and I are now the matriarchs of the family. We are, in fact, the end of the line, there is no 'next generation' to follow. Over the years we have each inherited items of jewellery from previous generations that neither of us wear. Now there is no one to hold the family history embedded in those items.

The topic of Jen's last blog from Bhutan was impermanence. As she was reflecting on the closure of her seminal year in Bhutan news came through of the death of her beloved Nana in Durham, England. Instead of returning to Australia with Jordi, Jen flew to the UK to join her father for the funeral. The concept of impermanence relates not only to matters of life and death, but also ownership of 'things'. With Jennifer's advocacy in mind I thought about the heirloom jewellery and how we might acknowledge its impermanence.

In my first job in Australia, as the social worker in a community geriatric assessment team based in Wallsend, Newcastle, I worked alongside an Occupational Therapist whose husband is a manufacturing jeweller. In consultation with Derek those unwearable rings from past generations have been transformed into items of beautiful jewellery, one being a gold pendant shaped into an endless knot.

Part 2

The Tour

A World Premiere, Sydney

When I was learning how to become a 'lady', I seem to recall being told not to wear gold and silver jewellery together. On my neck is the gold endless knot pendant fashioned by Derek. In my ears are the silver earrings so specially given to me by Jen in Bhutan. Whether or not they indicate poor adoption of style, they are essential for me to wear today for the premiere performance of *Endless*. I am also wearing purple. It was Jordi's idea to invite those attending Jen's funeral to "wear a splash of purple". This was the colour of Jen's bridesmaids' dresses – and her wedding shoes! Among many things we shared, purple is our favourite colour.

I am rather nervous. We are at the Sydney Recital Hall in Angel Place on a Saturday afternoon for what is to be the World Premiere performance of *Endless*. This is the first official performance, and it is programmed to open the second half of the concert. Audience numbers are the highest in a long time (374 I would later discover).

Among them are Jordi's parents and Judith's friend May.

I have just heard Karin Schaupp and the Flinders Quartet perform the Carulli guitar concerto and a quintet by Castelnuovo-Tedesco. Both pieces were also performed at the Melbourne rehearsal three weeks ago. In addition, Karin played a delightful solo by Australian composer Richard Charlton called *Southern Cross Dreaming*. I am delighting in the music and the skills on display by these five musicians who I have been so privileged to meet.

During the interval I briefly connected with Carl — only our second time in person. The first was during a window of lifted restrictions in 2022 at a concert by the Omega Ensemble, in which one of his works, *Concord* was premiered. Ironically, although this piece was written after *Endless* it was able to be performed first. By chance, and my good fortune, that world premiere performance was in Newcastle City Hall. Most graciously Carl arranged to meet with Judith and me before the performance. We took him to the neighbouring building, formerly the Newcastle Council offices where Jennifer's father once worked, and now a five-star hotel with 360-degree views over the city and harbour. In his role as Artistic Director for Musica Viva I had occasionally seen Carl when he accompanied musicians to Newcastle, but to meet him personally was a thrill. The ease of our conversation and exchange of hugs was unexpected.

During the interval at the *Endless* premiere in Sydney Judith and I introduced Carl to May. Initially she didn't comprehend, but on Judith's explanation she broke the ice perfectly when she said "Oh, THE Carl Vine?!" Later Carl shared a whisky with May as the four of us enjoyed amicable conversation at a post-performance pub meal. My special connection with him had begun.

Thankfully Carl had told me that he would be introducing *Endless* from the stage. Back in our seats only three rows from the front, Judith and I each took a deep breath as he made his way to the lectern stage left. However, nothing could have prepared me for what he said, and how he introduced both Jennifer and the music. This is how I recorded it in my diary the following day:

> *Not only did he explain how he crafted the music to reflect Jennifer's work ethic, quiet strength and love of dancing the salsa, but he also spoke with the highest respect about the person she was, and the loss to the world by her death. It was as if Carl had known Jen well, especially in her adulthood, yet all this he gleaned from immersing himself in her Bhutanese blog – which he recommended to the audience to look up. Never before have I attended a concert where the music dedication has been so full*

At each subsequent concert Carl's words would form the preamble to the performance of *Endless*. When he wasn't there in person he asked Karin Schaupp to read the text he supplied to her, the text he subsequently read from so that he "wouldn't mess it up" as he said. Though I know how difficult it can be to deliver a speech without a script, it was his unscripted first presentation that I found most meaningful. Perhaps it was because it was my first hearing of his words, but it was also delivered from the heart. During his presentation he even made reference to how Jennifer's life had been taken "by a drug addled driver who was on the wrong side of the road". It was information that I hadn't discussed with him, but was apparently part of his detailed research process, and evidence of his attitude towards both the driver and Jen's needless loss. Each time I was taken aback by the massed intake of breath when the audience received this news.

With Covid awareness still strongly on everyone's minds it was uncertain how much interaction would be possible with the musicians during the tour. I consequently approached the tour with no expectations, happy that I had at least made their acquaintance at the rehearsal concert in Melbourne. I was therefore delighted to be invited to join Musica Viva staff and the musicians for refreshments following the premier performance on that Saturday afternoon. An area of armchairs around tables was made available at the Fullerton Hotel, the space that once was the central Post Office in Martin Place. In a conversation with Carl that afternoon he was remembering buying postage stamps at the long wooden counter that used to be within inches of where we were sitting.

Judith, her friend May and I were the only "outsiders" to be invited to the gathering, which was otherwise populated by the musicians, composer and Musica Viva personnel. It felt like an enormous privilege, and initially I was nervous about being in such elite company. My anxiety was quickly assuaged however, as all three of us were included in conversations in the most friendly and welcoming way. I enjoyed speaking with each of the musicians and was interested to hear how they were engaging with *Endless* having now rehearsed it with Carl, and made their first public performance. It was both amazing and delightful for me to hear that Karin Schaupp is often tuned in to spiritual energy and feels it strongly when playing *Endless*. A week or so later Zoe shared a similar experience with me. It brings me such delight knowing that Jen can share her beautiful spirit in this way, with those who are receptive to receiving it.

I am privileged to feel constantly surrounded by Jen's presence, but it is a blessing that she can, and does, share this with others.

At one point Anne Frankenberg, Musica Viva CEO, perched on the arm of my lounge chair. I had given Anne a copy of Jennifer's book *Eighteen* following a concert at Admiralty House just before Christmas. The concert was one of many privileges I have been given due to this association with Musica Viva. Judith and I found ourselves included in a December invitation to hear a song recital at Admiralty House as guests of the Governor General and his wife. It was a private recital for benefactors of Musica Viva, to which I, as commissioner of *Endless,* and Judith as Concert Champion for both Sydney and Newcastle concerts, were included. It was one of those warm, windy days of early summer, so we both look windswept in the photos we took from the grounds with Sydney Harbour as a backdrop and the Opera House directly opposite. As post-concert drinks and canapes were served on the back veranda, I was engaged in conversation with a gentleman who, within minutes, was also sharing his experience of loss. His wife had recently died. As a medical practitioner he recommended a new book "The Grieving Brain", which I subsequently acquired online. I found it a fascinating explanation of how brain activity changes as a result of grief. I felt drawn to find the gentleman who had given me this helpful recommendation, but hesitated to engage in what might be perceived as internet trolling.

It was at the Admiralty House recital where I met Anne Frankenberg. She was just commencing in the role of CEO of Musica Viva. I had signed the contract for the commission with her predecessor, Hywel Syms in August 2021. I met Hywel at Admiralty House, the day before he left Australia for his new assignment in America. Anne, formerly his deputy, was taking the reins. As it turned out, the *Endless* tour would be the first for Anne as CEO. It was another of my somewhat impulsive acts to offer Anne a copy of *Eighteen* that day. I later felt a little awkward about having done so, even though I was keen to share Jennifer's story as widely as I could. Any doubts were assuaged when, from her perch on my armchair at the Fullerton, she told me how inspired she was to read it and that she had already loaned the book to the musicians who were taking turns to read it. My heart sang. Here was another audience keen to fill out their understanding of Jen. I made sure that each of the musicians, as well as Carl, received their own copy of *Eighteen*. So they didn't need to carry extra weight in their luggage, in addition to their instruments, I delivered copies to each of them when they were in their home city – Carl and Thibaud in Sydney, Zoe, Wilma and Helen in

Melbourne, and Karin in Brisbane.

I subsequently met Anne at most of the concerts on the tour and developed a deepening connection. During her interval speeches, introducing herself as the new CEO to subscribers and distinguished guests, she held my hand as she acknowledged Jen and the commissioning process of *Endless*. She made every attempt to include purple in her costume choices for the concerts in honour of Jen's favourite colour. And during the final performance of *Endless* in Adelaide she reached out to me as my shoulders shook and my tears fell. It had been beautifully thoughtful of Viv, one of several new members of the Musica Viva staff who I met during the tour, to swap my seat allocation so I sat beside Anne for that final performance. It was one of only two concerts I attended without Judith's company. Sitting directly in front of us in the Dress Circle of the Adelaide Town Hall was South Australia's Governor, Her Excellency, the Honourable Frances Adamson. I had been introduced to her during the interval, and as she turned around to acknowledge me during the applause for *Endless* both Anne and I had handkerchiefs to our eyes.

Newcastle

The Newcastle concert was always going to be the most important of the tour for me. Being Jennifer's hometown, and a venue I frequently attended, I knew there would be many people with connections to Jen or me. Additionally, in the lead-up to the concerts in both 2022 and 2023 I had contacted as many of our friends as possible, hers and mine, to let them know about the tour venues - and of course the 2022 postponement. While it was delightful to catch up with friends in celebration of Jen in Sydney, Canberra and Melbourne, it was the concert in Newcastle's City Hall where so many people with connections to Jen would throng.

Although the refurbishment of the Newcastle Conservatorium Harold Lobb Concert Hall had been completed, it was no longer available to Musica Viva, so concerts continued to be performed in Newcastle City Hall. It is a fine venue with significantly larger seating capacity than the conservatorium. Due to continued Covid anxiety the few concerts that had been able to be delivered during 2022 had smaller audiences than usual, and I felt uncomfortable on behalf of the performers in City Hall's sparsely filled cavernous space. I had recently joined the Newcastle Musica Viva committee and much of the discussion in 2022 was about building audience numbers. The move to City Hall's larger venue necessitated this, let alone the continued impact of Covid. So, imagine my delight when, during a committee Zoom meeting the week before the Newcastle concert, an announcement was made about seat bookings. Numbers for the concert were so high that, had we remained at the Harold Lobb Concert Hall, it would already have sold out!

I wanted to offer some special friends an opportunity to meet and greet over a drink and snack prior to the concert. I had established that Carl would be able to attend Newcastle, though he would be unavailable to stay beyond the performance due to teaching commitments in Sydney the following morning. He would, however, be available prior to the concert, and I was keen for him to meet some of Jen's friends, and mine. With wonderful assistance from Musica Viva, a reception was arranged for the hour prior to the concert, located in a corner of the ground floor bar of City Hall. As it had been my idea to provide the refreshments, I anticipated collecting the cost. Again, I was humbled by Musica Viva taking responsibility for all costs and arrangements. The hour itself felt like a flurry of greetings and introductions, an activity that induces high levels of stress for me as I am innately shy and notably bad at remembering names. For the most part I was clutching a bouquet of four enormous chrysanthemums, their petals a mix of purple and white, presented to me, to my utmost surprise, by Scott Bevan.

Not only was there a pre-concert reception in Newcastle, but afterwards Musica Viva hosted another reception, this one open to all subscribers as well as my special invitees. When I was making arrangements with Musica Viva staffer Caroline for the Newcastle receptions, she was not able to confirm if the musicians would be joining the post-concert gathering. Having met with them in Sydney after the premiere performance I remained hopeful. My wishes were granted and all five performers graced the occasion. In another of those interconnections, so aptly symbolised by the endless knot, a remarkable reconnection was made. Many years prior, the young journalist Scott Bevan had interviewed a budding guitarist Karin Schaupp, the occasion remembered by both. Their reunion that evening was a delight to observe.

Adding a layer of anxiety to my already adrenaline-filled body, Anne had invited me to 'say a few words' at the post-concert reception. She had given me 24 hours to think about it, and though it presented such a good opportunity for me to publicly acknowledge the support I have received, I was uncertain if I could manage it. I was, however, determined to give it my best shot. I have the dot-point notes that I referred to that evening, but I have no recollection of what I said. In a way perhaps the writing of this memoir is an effort to expand my expression of gratitude. Everyone I have so far mentioned, and many more besides, have been fundamental to the success of the *Endless* journey, not only for me, but also for the music.

It is hardly surprising that I don't recall my speech. Moments earlier I had heard cellist Zoe make her announcement from the stage. At each venue, at the conclusion of the programmed pieces, the musicians returned to the stage to acknowledge the sustained applause. They then took their seats again as Zoe thanked everyone for clapping so they 'got to play the encore'. In Newcastle it was the third time I had heard Zoe's introduction, but hearing it in a room where so many people knew me felt far more exposing than the relative anonymity of the two Sydney concerts thus far.

The encore piece they were about to play was *Salsa Falsa*. During our email correspondence in 2021 I had asked Carl about extending my commission to add a short piece that could be played as an encore. I suggested a guitar solo, thinking it to be a less demanding extra assignment for Carl. His response email came within the hour. Counter-intuitively, he said, writing for solo guitar is more complex, not less, than writing for a quintet. What he also told me was that in the process of writing *Endless* he was obliged to "excise" a section. He described his excision as "really sweet", befitting a tour encore, and that he would work on it for that purpose – with no extra fee!

In late 2021, shortly after I had received the manuscript for *Endless,* another postal delivery brought the score for the encore, *Salsa Falsa.* It too bears a huge endless knot symbol on both the title page and beneath the Program Note inside. This time I was not privy to Carl's script prior to publication. It reads:

> **Salsa Falsa** *first emerged as part of my guitar quintet* Endless. *That work required a celebratory salsa for which* Falsa *was the first unsuccessful attempt. My local specialist in all music South American, Daniel Rojas, assured me that it didn't qualify as salsa in any meaningful way and was, at best, some sort of perverse tango. At the urging of Kathryn Bennett, who commissioned* Endless, *I distilled that abortive exercise into this short concert encore as a falsa sort of salsa. It is dedicated to Kathryn.*

Furthermore, Carl signed the manuscript with a beautiful personal message to me.

Wow!!

Back on stage prior to playing *Salsa Falsa,* Zoe's announcement acknowledged the long wait for the concert to be delivered, the musicians' appreciation for Musica Viva, the joy of performing with Karin Schaupp, and that *Salsa Falsa* had emerged from *Endless.* Before lifting her bow to start playing she also added "it is dedicated to Jen's mum, Kathryn."

Wow again!

I wrote in my diary that night:

> *That is totally how I want to be described and remembered.*

As if two 'wows' were not enough, by the time the concert arrived in Canberra, Zoe had added a couple more lines to her speech. Not only did she comment about how I had been attending all the concerts, but that I have "become a friend to the musicians".

Again I refer to my diary note for that night:

> *It is one thing for me to feel this beautiful friendship with the musicians, it's another level to know that it is reciprocated, but it's quite something else for it to*

be made so public as to be shared with a concert hall

full of people.

Zoe shared that same message for the rest of the tour!

45

Melbourne

A couple of times at the end of the concert some of the musicians were invited to return to the stage for a post-concert interview. In Melbourne the interviewer was Paul Kildea, Artistic Director of Musica Viva. In turn he asked questions of Carl, Karin and Wilma. At this point I hadn't really connected with Paul, having met him only briefly in Newcastle. I anticipated high-brow questions about musicology but instead Paul was keen to ask about *Endless*. He explored how its process both honours Jen's life and provides a rare addition to the guitar repertoire. It seems that this piece is super-special to guitarists, and Paul is confident it will become a sought-after piece for performance. There are, apparently, very few works for guitar and string quartet. One of the questions from the audience was specifically about how Carl approached the commission. This resulted in him sharing even more about Jen. My diary entry that day best summarises my reaction:

I am totally overwhelmed by how central Jen is to this whole concert tour, and how significantly she is touching the hearts of audiences.

Over post-concert refreshments in Melbourne I had the opportunity to spend time with Paul and established a great rapport. By coincidence he has connections with Maitland, his family home being in Steam Street. He too is deeply moved by Jen's story and my commission, and in particular the confluence of circumstances that enabled him to commission a work from Carl. On each subsequent meeting I have been greeted by Paul with a hug and a kiss, once even in front of Her Excellency Frances Adamson in Adelaide, whose Covid protocol continued to utilise elbow bumps as a form of greeting. It created a moment of "oops" followed by shared laughter.

While in Melbourne I had hoped to catch up with Maryanne, the hostess of the 'house concert' radio prize. I had made a special connection with her. Just prior to our afternoon flight home the day after that rehearsal concert, Judith and I had a stroll through the Botanic Gardens. We were about to ask a trio of women walking ahead of us if they could direct us to the café, when one of them turned and approached us with a greeting on her lips. It was Maryanne! In the vastness of the Botanic

Gardens, let alone Melbourne, the only person we knew in town was in exactly the same spot. As we walked with them through the park towards the café I was in deep conversation with Maryanne. She told me how it would soon be the first anniversary of the death of her mother, how close they had been and how deeply she misses her. It was like we started chatting mid-sentence, not needing any preamble but making instant sense to each other through our experiences of grief. Without fear of being misjudged we were even able to share the quirky things that we notice, things that we believe to be indicators of other-worldly connections. In Maryanne's case it is random flowers that pop up in her garden from a mother who was an avid gardener. In mine it is the appearance of dragonflies, my long-held totem of our interconnectedness with the afterlife. It reminded me of my experience with the gentleman at Admiralty House who recommended I read *The Grieving Brain*. It was as if Jen's story and *Endless* have become passports to a land of shared loss. Throughout the tour people continued to share their experience of grief with me. It is for this reason that I have chosen to take this story to a wider audience, to acknowledge the significance of loss in all our lives, and to give it an avenue for expression.

I first met Imelda when she approached the Rotary Club I belonged to in Maitland, expressing an interest in the project that I coordinated. She offered her services as a videographer to record our trip to Vanuatu in 2015. The project was to assist a village school to catch and collect rainwater from the classroom roofs. The video that Imelda created was an excellent resource for our club to promote the community development approach for which I strongly advocated. Sadly with Jennifer's death came my incapacity to continue with the project, and as a Rotarian. Over tapas in one of Melbourne's laneways, having reconnected at the concert the previous evening, Imelda and I renewed our friendship and recalled some highlights from that trip as well as our responses to *Endless*. In telling her how the *Endless* project came about, Imelda encouraged me to write about it in such a way that it sounded like it was an inevitable outcome. She fired my interest, and the following morning I awoke with the imagery of the Bhutanese gift shop, buying the silver endless knot earrings with Jen. I had my starting point.

I also reconnected with Aruna, one of Jennifer's bridesmaids, who was her fellow volunteer and flatmate in the Philippines in 2006. It was my first opportunity to meet Aruna's husband Sonu. A musician himself, Sonu was unable to attend the *Endless* concert as he was rehearsing with his band for their upcoming tour. When Jen and Jordi were in Bhutan for a year, Aruna and Sonu lived in Mumbai. The four of them spent Christmas together in India. That was when Jen delivered her wedding gift to them, an intricately carved wooden endless knot to which Jen added her special words of wedding greeting. This was a story I had not previously heard, nor had I seen the photo that Sonu subsequently shared with me, of Jen with the Bhutanese craftsman holding his endless knot carving. It was another confirmation of just how significant the endless knot symbol is to, and for, Jen, and how appropriate it is that Carl's composition bears its title.

Canberra

In the later stages of planning for the concert performances I approached Musica Viva with an inquiry about stage lighting. I had been inspired by an online concert (the only type we could watch at the time) of Genevieve Lacey and Marshall McGuire which featured some spectacularly beautiful lighting. I asked if the performances of *Endless* might be able to have purple lighting to reflect Jen's purple passion. With no promises given as to the outcome, my request was considerately acknowledged, the final result needing to rely on what would be available at each of the eight venues. What I observed was a brave attempt to change the lighting atmosphere for each performance of *Endless*, in most cases giving it a purple haze. The stand-out achievement was at Llewellyn Hall in Canberra. Within its brutalist concrete structure, a curved timber screen cradled the performance space. In addition to any acoustic advantages, it also provided a backdrop for pillars of up-lights, which, during *Endless,* were a stunning purple.

While in Canberra we visited the Yarralumla peninsula

and specifically a memorial to the 2001 Siev X disaster. It is an installation of 353 totem poles, each one representing a mother, father or child, whose life was lost as they tried to escape from Saddam Hussein's regime in Iraq. The poles, taller for adults, shorter for children, are Koppers logs decorated by communities around Australia to represent the life lost. Most remain unnamed. Tragically these families lost not only their lives but also their identity. I wept. I was stunned by the total contrast with my *Endless* journey and how it holds Jennifer as its focal point. My privilege is to offer Jennifer's memory and legacy to the world. The experience of these people was a total loss of privilege, of homeland, of security, of human rights, and even their identity. Each totem pole could represent a person who shared some of Jennifer's attributes. The experience was visceral.

In addition to the official Musica Viva tour program were a couple of additional concerts. The musicians travelled to Hobart between the two Melbourne performances and included a road trip to Nowra following Canberra. I didn't include these extra venues in my itinerary as I didn't think I would have the stamina. At the outset, one of the things I was keen to learn about was how musicians approach a performance tour. By the time the tour reached Canberra it was confirmed for me how exhausting it can be. I shared my observations with the musicians one evening, acknowledging that all I had to do was to sit and listen. By contrast they had not only to perform, but also to practice, undertake lengthy sound checks, as well as be interviewed or hold masterclasses – or both! Needless to say, my appreciation for all musicians on tour, but especially the five wonderful people on this Musica Viva tour, has increased inordinately.

A measure of Karin's connection with the endless knot symbolism was the communication she sent me following their Nowra performance. Not having my contact details at that stage, she sent an email to me via Carl. It was a selfie photo of her with a Nowra audience member, Eva. It turns out that Eva was at the concert by coincidence and had no prior knowledge about the piece or its meaning. She was surprised to be hearing a familiar story when Carl's notes were read on stage by Karin. As a close friend of Jordi's mother, Eva was keenly aware of Jen and her tragic death. At the post-concert reception in Newcastle I had a similar experience. A subscriber, unaware of the program prior to the concert, approached me following my speech and introduced herself as an architect and former colleague of Jen's. They had worked together at a local architecture firm during Jen's early career. As Carl added to the email that he forwarded from Karin, "talk about interconnectedness!!!"

Brisbane

Griffith University, located on Brisbane's South Bank, struck me as a most vibrant place of musical education. On a Tuesday evening I watched as the crowd swelled prior to the concert hall doors opening. I was impressed by the large number of students who emerged from practice rooms. Many were inquiring about the availability of tickets for the concert, and most of them had "Karin Schaupp" on their lips. This is where Karin teaches her craft, and she is obviously held in high regard. I was alone this time – no Judith, no Anne, no Paul, and no Carl yet – though he did arrive in time to introduce *Endless* from the stage. I also felt a bit self-conscious on my own during the interval drinks to which I was invited, where, without Anne to give her speech, it was just a gathering of subscribers. Why should I be surprised, then, when the only person I spoke with turned out to be a lady who was born in Tadcaster, the place in Yorkshire where I attended Grammar School? That ubiquitous endless knot!

When Zoe invited me to be an observer at her Master

Class I jumped at this unique opportunity. It took place the morning after the concert in a room below the concert hall at Griffith University. In turn, two quartets received her tuition for about 45 minutes each. First they played the piece of music they had selected for her analysis. Zoe then addressed different passages with them. One quartet was an unusual combination of piano, violin, cello and clarinet. The piece they played was the *Quartet for the End of Time* by Messiaen, music he composed when he was in a concentration camp, and these were the only instruments available. Having explained this Zoe asked one of the quartet to describe the music. She then asked him to express what he had just said by the way he played it. What a powerful way of teaching. Once again, my own learning curve experienced a big upturn. The multitude of nuances within a single piece of music is quite phenomenal. Not only did the two quartets benefit from Zoe's tuition, but there was a room full of other music students. From my seat at the back of the room I counted over 90 young people squashed into the room. Wearing outfits ranging from thongs to Doc Martens, skimpy tops and shorts to sloppy oversized things, every one of them was totally focussed throughout the class. I left the room not only feeling privileged at this great opportunity, but also reassured that the future of music is in good hands.

By pure chance, and for the only time, the musicians and I were on the same flight from Brisbane to Adelaide. After checking in our luggage, minus the precious instruments that stayed close to the musicians at all times, Thibaud invited everyone to the Virgin Lounge. As a member of a Melbourne quartet, this Sydneysider's travelling lifestyle has amassed numerous frequent flyer perks, and this one he shared with us all. To be accepted as part of the group was such a joy once again, especially now that I was without Judith's company. To my surprise, as we enjoyed the free refreshments, Karin gave me a ribbon-wrapped gift.

In the foyer of the Queensland Conservatorium following the performance the previous evening, Karin had been excited to introduce me to her husband, daughter and son. It felt like another beautiful gift of friendship. The image of Karin and 14-year-old Alexa, their heads together with identically joyous expressions on their faces, exactly as Jen and I used to do, gave me a moment of deep connection with mother and daughter.

Shortly afterwards Karin waved the family off in their car and joined us for post-concert celebrations. This included Thibaud, Wilma, Helen and Zoe of the Flinders Quartet, Carl (on what was to be his last concert of this tour), and several musical colleagues and students of Karin. We walked along the South Bank in search of a place large enough to accommodate a group of twenty or so, and one that was not about to close at 10pm. This was one of the unanticipated outcomes of Covid, a result of staff shortages, with an impact on socialising that stretched beyond the lockdown limitations. Although surrounded by people whose lives and livelihoods are far from my range of familiarity, at no time did I feel any awkwardness or exclusion. My diary captures its essence thus:

> *I can't overemphasise the privilege it is for me to be part of such occasions, and to see professional musicians doing what they do with others in their profession. Rather than a fly on the wall I have been warmly included. I even feel at times venerated for the small part I have played in this process. It is such a good example of planting a seed and watching it grow. Mine was only the seed of commissioning something to be written in honour of Jen. Everyone else has nurtured the process into the incredible tour that is under way, and mine is the joy to observe its development.*

On Brisbane's South Bank that evening I received another surprise. Together Carl and Karin told me that they had been discussing the possibility of transcribing *Endless* into a guitar concerto – in other words, to be played with an orchestra instead of a string quartet. It would, they told me, expand its potential repertoire. This was certainly another left field delivery. Though neither of them could give any promises about the outcome, their consideration of it is evidence of the endlessness of this journey. Who knows where else it could take us?

In the airport lounge before we headed to Adelaide, the final destination of the tour, I untied the ribbon of Karin's gift. It was a trio of CDs, each featuring different aspects of her musical recordings. One is a 2011 recording with the Flinders Quartet featuring the Boccherini *Fandango* that is also being performed on this tour. The cover image shows Karin with Zoe and Helen, foundation members of the Flinders Quartet, with two different violinists. Wilma joined the quartet most recently, and Thibaud is about to leave. In fact, the Adelaide performance will be his last official concert as a member of the Flinders Quartet. During the tour I spoke with him about his decision to leave, and future plans. His first assignment, only a few days after Adelaide, is to visit Europe in search of a new violin.

One of the people who joined us at the South Bank restaurant was Umberto Clerici, the new chief conductor of the Queensland Symphony Orchestra. Unfortunately, he was unable to attend the *Endless* concert as he was in rehearsal with the orchestra. Umberto is not only a close friend of Karin's, but also a playing partner, their duets forming the content of one of my CD gifts. Prior to becoming a conductor Umberto was a solo cellist. When I shook his hand that evening I wasn't to know that he would also become a regular guest in my loungeroom, as I listen to him play on the *Wayfaring* CD with Karin.

Perhaps the most poignant of my CD trilogy gift is the one called *Cradle Songs*. It features lullabies from around the world, adapted as guitar solos. Karin created it for Alexa when she was a baby, and it is her image that adorns the cover. Having met Alexa the previous evening, this gift is more than its music – it is a beautiful connection to Karin and her family.

Adelaide

The Adelaide concert was special for several reasons. Each year the Adelaide Festival brings widely varied performances to the city, attracting huge interest and audiences. Musica Viva had aligned their ticketing for the Adelaide concert with the Festival, and as a result ticket sales were higher than anywhere else. Here over 600 people simultaneously drew breath upon hearing how Jennifer's life had been taken. They also sat in silence for several seconds before erupting in rapturous applause following the performance of *Endless*. Early in the tour Judith had started counting the seconds of silence that followed each performance and told me the longest was six seconds. I think this one was longer. The passionate journey that Carl's music delivers, together with the meaning within which it is wrapped, deeply resonated with every audience, requiring time for emotional rebalancing before expressing their appreciation. That is, with the exception of the evening concert in Sydney. I watched a band of admiring young students surround Carl during the interval, and after hearing *Endless* they were keen to express their appreciation of their mentor by braking into immediate applause.

Adelaide was a farewell concert for Thibaud with the Flinders Quartet. I had so enjoyed his sonorous playing, not just of *Endless* but of all the tour repertoire. Observing the musicians across eight performances gave me the opportunity to watch more deeply how they create their musical magic. On stage they project an easy mutual understanding, demonstrated by subtle leadership cues. It suggests a team where equality is celebrated. It creates a stage presence without undue distraction. As Zoe added to her on-stage speech prior to the *Salsa Falsa* encore that evening, she had a tear in her eye that this was their final performance with Thibaud. That said, what I noticed about the Adelaide performance was that it flowed with greater ease than any of the others. The musicians later acknowledged that they all felt more relaxed, due not only to their familiarity with the music, but anticipating the end of the tour. Sadly, this performance was not recorded. That was the one I most wanted to bottle!

One concert was recorded however – and that was the Sydney evening performance attended by Carl's rapturous students. The following Saturday, 4 March, it was broadcast as a Lunchtime Concert on ABC Classic. I was pleased to have this opportunity to share *Endless* with friends overseas, and others who couldn't make it to a concert, by providing details of the radio broadcast and access to the website link afterwards. Most importantly the lunchtime broadcast gave me an opportunity to hear the concert in my own loungeroom. This was the weekend I was at home, between Canberra and Brisbane. My diary entry captures the emotion of that moment:

> *I had been looking forward to this because I knew that I needed to be able to express myself while listening to Endless in a way that sitting in a concert hall with its required decorum does not allow. Increasingly the salsa theme in Endless undoes me, as I feel the rhythm and connect with how Jen enjoyed dancing. So on Saturday lunchtime I sat with the box of tissues beside me and let myself howl. This was a rare opportunity for me to revisit that submerged chasm of deepest grief and devastating loss. It is a selfish emotion that I try to hold at bay, but it also needs its expression and release, and Saturday provided that opportunity.*

As befitted the end of a highly successful tour, there was an after-party in Adelaide. This time it was held in a private home, a relaxed setting for the musicians to unwind over drinks and eats. It was also an opportunity for Anne to summarise this, her first tour as CEO of Musica Viva, and to express her thanks to various people. Once again she drew attention to me. She said that this tour had been like none previously in relation to the connection with the commission, the emotional content of the music and the fact that I had attended each concert. This was another revelation to me. In my naivety I would have expected that greater things had previously occurred with people with deeper musical connections and influence than me.

It was at the Adelaide after-party where I met Adrian, Anne's husband. A few more dots were joined – or perhaps I should say threads, as this is so much related to the interconnectedness of the endless knot and how its influence has infused my whole *Endless* experience. Adrian, a former opera singer, is now the Managing Director of radio station 3MBS in Melbourne. It was 3MBS subscriber Maryanne who hosted the 'house concert' in the Lutheran Church, the gift of the Flinders Quartet. In expressing her thanks to the radio station for her win, Maryanne asked them to contact me for information about Jen so that it could be included in their promotion of the upcoming Musica Viva tour. It had been Adrian's name on the bottom of the email I received asking for some background information. In shaking his hand at the after-party I had one of those 'aha' moments as everything slotted into place.

I also reconnected with none other than the gentleman who, at Admiralty House in Sydney, told me about *The Grieving Brain*. I had hoped I might encounter him at one of the Sydney concerts as I was keen to thank him for his book recommendation. It was a total surprise to see him here, so far away from his Sydney home. He was in Adelaide for the Festival and told me that he was about to attend concerts at Ukaria, a purpose-built chamber music venue in the Adelaide Hills.

Earlier, as we sat beside each other in the Dress Circle of Adelaide Town Hall prior to the concert, Anne and I were talking about life after the tour. Anne will return to living between Sydney and Melbourne, the latter her family home, the former the headquarters of Musca Viva. But first she would be taking in some of the offerings of the Adelaide Festival, now approaching its 2023 conclusion. My plan, I explained, was to stay in Adelaide for a further five days to process the enormity of the past few weeks of the *Endless* tour. When planning my trip I knew I would need time to rest and gather my emotional equilibrium before returning home and picking up 'normal' life, so I had extended my stay in Adelaide accordingly. Upon hearing that I would still be in Adelaide over the weekend she immediately texted Paul Kildea, whose seat was elsewhere in the Town Hall. Anne had just asked Paul to return to Sydney to meet with significant Musica Viva benefactors for an unexpected opportunity. Consequently, he could not make use of tickets he had purchased for concerts at Ukaria. To my delight, at the North Adelaide house, Paul gave me a folder of three tickets for the Saturday and Sunday concerts. His gift came with the warmest of hugs and kind words. Not only did I get to attend these intimate and exquisite performances, but it also enabled further connection with the gentleman I became invited to call Andrew.

The tour was over, but my *Endless* journey continued.

There is no place to finish an endless story. The journey I embarked on in 2021 with an email to Nigel Westlake was not its beginning. Nor does my return home from Adelaide on 15 March 2023 mark its end. It has delivered countless new experiences and reminded me of many challenges. I have made new friendships and learned a lot more about myself. I have introduced Jennifer to countless people and met many who share the pain of grief. All of these threads have the capacity for further development, to be interwoven with other threads creating an intricate fabric, a continuing *Endless* story. Perhaps my diary entry, written on 3 March, at Canberra airport, while awaiting a long-delayed flight back to Newcastle, sums it up best:

> *I can only feel that my Endless journey is the gift that keeps on giving.*

Thanks

To all those I have met on *My Endless Journey* I offer my sincere gratitude. We now have endless connections in, and through, Jennifer and music.

To Carl Vine, my deepest thanks for representing Jennifer in music, and for interpreting her essence so well. I feel you have got to know my daughter and have become one of her champions. For this I hold you very dear.

To the musicians, Karin Schaupp and the Flinders Quartet members Thibaud Pavlovic-Hobba, Wilma Smith, Helen Ireland and Zoe Knighton, it was my privilege to observe you at your work, delivering music exquisitely. The bonds that we made during the tour are truly an unanticipated gift and deeply treasured.

The support of Musica Viva Australia has been fundamental to the entire development of the commission and its delivery as a series of concerts. To Hywel Syms and Anne Frankenberg as leaders of the organisation, and Artistic Director Paul Kildea, together with their team including Katherine Kemp, Zoe Cobden-Jewitt, Caroline

Davis, Justine Nguyen and Viv Rosman my heartfelt thanks for the warmth you brought to all our interactions. Musica Viva really is an Australian treasure.

My thanks to Nigel Westlake for the wisdom of your recommendation to approach Musica Viva, and to Maryanne Molenaar for inviting me to the 'house concert' that gave me my introduction to *Endless* and to the musicians.

To Scott Bevan I extend my gratitude for supporting me to honour Jennifer, your heart-felt radio interview that gave publicity to the Newcastle concert, and for the purple flowers!

For encouraging me to put my story into writing I thank Imelda Cooney, and for editing I appreciate the assistance of Debbie Lee.

Without Graham Davidson my writing would remain as a Word document. Thank you for your expertise in creating this handsome book.

To all those I have named in my story, and to the many who were part of the journey but are not referred to directly, you have all contributed to the creation of wonderful memories. I am endlessly grateful to you all.

My sister Judith has been by my side throughout this journey, both at the concerts and in helping me prepare this memoir. It is her photography that enhances the book, and her constant support that enabled me to achieve this project. My heart is full of sisterly love for you, Judith.

Jennifer, my darling daughter, remains my greatest source of blessings. On this journey she has delivered countless gifts. Now, through *Endless,* her legacy lives in music. Thanks, Jen, for what you were, are, and will be. Endlessly.

Immortalising Joy

by Justine Nguyen

How do we honour and hold close the memory of loved ones who have passed away? How do we seek to immortalise the joy they have brought into our lives, so precious and often difficult to capture?

For longstanding subscriber Kathryn Bennett, approaching Musica Viva Australia to commission a work in tribute to her late, beloved daughter Jennifer Bates was one such way. Both mother and daughter shared a deep love of music, Jennifer an avid salsa dancer and chorister. In fact, the evening before her death in an accident in 2016, Jennifer had attended a rehearsal with the community choir of which she was a member, Stella A Cappella. In a text message to her mother, Jennifer described the experience as 'nice and uplifting'.

Both are words many would use to describe Jennifer herself, a 36-year-old award-winning architect and passionate environmentalist who was embedded in the Newcastle community. Promoted to senior project manager of the NSW Public Works Department in Newcastle days before her death, she had also won a Women in Building Award a few months earlier.

Jennifer's keen environmentalism saw her serve as the coordinator of the Newcastle chapter of Beyond Zero Emissions, a national climate change solutions think-tank, and one of her final projects was overseeing the installation of solar panels at a Public Works office.

What leisure time Jennifer had she devoted to her artistic pursuits - she met her husband Jordi after they both attended a salsa class in Sydney. This love of salsa she brought to locals in Bhutan where she and Jordi spent twelve months as volunteers for the Australian government. During this time, she completed her Master's degree, helped to coordinate an inaugural cultural festival, and became immersed in the Bhutanese culture and Buddhist philosophy.

These are just a few aspects of her daughter's rich life that Kathryn shared with composer Carl Vine. Musica Viva Australia's Artistic Director from 2000 to 2019, Carl was already engaged by the company to write a piece for Karin Schaupp to perform in the 2022 season. When Kathryn approached MVA about a commission to honour Jennifer's memory in 2021, Carl was delighted to combine the two ideas into one work. Initially programmed for Schaupp and Flinders Quartet to perform as part of the first tour of MVAs 2022 season, it makes its long-awaited world premiere in this concert tour.

Further communications between Kathryn and Carl helped shape the final work, *Endless*. The name is a nod to the symbolic knot significant in Buddhism, representing among many things the cycle of birth, death and rebirth; the intertwining of wisdom and compassion; and the interconnectedness of all things. For Kathryn, the endless knot represents the enduring connection between herself and Jennifer, whose experiences in Bhutan proved life-changing. It was in a letter to Carl that Kathryn first mentioned the symbol's importance to mother and daughter, which Carl has alluded to in the interweaving musical lines of his piece.

Above all, *Endless* is a celebration of Jennifer's life, a mother's way of remembering the joy her daughter imparted, and the contribution she made, in the time she was given. The commissioning process has been a very positive one for Kathryn, who has appreciated the opportunity to reflect upon and share memories of her daughter. The performances are opportunities to continue Jennifer's contribution to the world.

As Kathryn wrote to Carl, 'Jen was, and remains, my best friend - a wonderful privilege for me as a mother.'